ROUGHAGE DIET

Effects Of Feeding Roughages As Expander Extruded Diets

Elizabeth K. Poole

Table of Contents

CHAPTER ONE

ROUGHAGE DIET

ROUGHAGE AND ITS IMPORTANT TO OUR HEALTH

Wellbeing specialists have long suggested consuming roughage, generally called fiber, to work on stomach related wellbeing.

Roughage is the part of plant food varieties, like entire grains, nuts, seeds, vegetables, natural products, and vegetables that your body can't process.

Be that as it may, it's a significant food hotspot for the advantageous microorganisms in your stomach. It might likewise help weight the executives and diminishing specific gamble factors for coronary illness.

This article makes sense of what roughage is, audits its advantages, and gives a rundown of roughage-rich food sources.

WHAT IS ROUGHAGE

Roughage, or fiber, alludes to the crabs in plants that your body can't process. This article utilizes the terms roughage and fiber conversely.

When roughage arrives at your digestive organ, it's either

separated by your stomach microbes or ways out your body in your stools.

Two primary sorts of fiber

- Dissolvable
- Insoluble

Dissolvable fiber

Most food sources high in roughage contain a blend of these yet are normally more extravagant in one sort.

In the stomach, solvent fiber assimilates water to become gel-like. This permits your stomach microscopic organisms to separate it without any problem. Chiai seeds and oats are both high in solvent fiber.

Insoluble fiber

Interestingly, insoluble fiber has a more inflexible tiny design and doesn't assimilate water. All things considered, it adds mass to stools. Products of the soil contain high measures of insoluble fiber.

You ought to attempt to eat 14 grams of fiber for each 1,000 calories you consume each day. That is around 25 grams for ladies and 38 grams for men. Sadly, just around 5% of individuals arrive at this proposal.

Not eating sufficient fiber can adversely influence your wellbeing. For instance, eating an eating regimen low in fiber has been connected to stomach related issues like blockage and advantageous interaction, which is the unusual development of hurtful microscopic organisms in the stomach

Counts calories low in fiber is likewise connected with an expanded gamble of weight, colon disease, and bosom malignant growth.

CHAPTER TWO

ADVANTAGES OF ROUGHAGE

You might have heard that adding roughage to your eating routine can work on your assimilation.

Without a doubt, roughage meaningfully affects your stomach, like expanding the majority of stools, diminishing obstruction, and taking care of advantageous stomach microorganisms.

Food sources high in roughage are likewise normally more extravagant in nutrients, minerals, and cell reinforcements than low-fiber food sources like refined grains. Furthermore, they might even assist you with getting in shape.

Roughage further develops assimilation and stomach wellbeing

Dietary fiber assumes a wide range of parts in stomach wellbeing.

Insoluble fiber mitigates clogging by adding mass to stools, while the gel-like consistency of solvent fiber helps move stools all the more effectively through your intestinal system.

One review in north of 62,000 ladies found that the people who ate somewhere around 20 grams of fiber day to day were significantly less prone to encounter blockage than the individuals who ate just 7 grams or less each day.

One more review in 51 individuals investigated the impacts of eating fiber on obstruction. Consistently for quite some time, members ate 240 grams of bread - either rye or white. The rye bread contained 30 grams of fiber, while the white bread contained 10 grams.

Contrasted with the white-bread bunch, the rye-bread bunch encountered a 23% quicker travel season of defecations, 1.4 more solid discharges each week, and gentler stools that passed all the more effectively.

Dietary fiber additionally goes about as a pre-biotic, which takes care of the gainful supportive of biotic microscopic organisms in your stomach, empowering them to flourish and restrict the development of unsafe microorganisms.

The pre-biotic in fiber may likewise diminish your gamble of colon disease by advancing sound defecations and reinforcing the layer of tissue coating your digestion tracts.

Roughage assists you with dealing with your weight

Consuming fiber may likewise help you reach and keep a sound weight.

In one review, 28 grown-ups expanded their fiber admission from 16 to 28 grams each day. They followed one of two high-fiber eats less carbs day to day for a long time - either 1.5 cups of beans or a mix of natural products, vegetables, and entire grains.

On both high-fiber eats less carbs members at around 300 less calories each day and shed around 3 pounds on normal simultaneously, they announced more elevated levels of totality and less craving than before they began the high-fiber diet.

Eating more fiber may likewise build your resting metabolic rate (RMR), which is the quantity of calories you consume very still.

A 6-week study in 81 grown-ups found that the people who ate an eating regimen containing around 40 grams of fiber everyday had a higher RMR and consumed 92 additional calories each day, contrasted with the individuals who ate an eating regimen with something like 21 grams of fiber each day.

Moreover, some high-fiber food varieties, like entire products of the soil, are low in calories. Take a stab at eating a greater amount of these food varieties to feel full and fulfilled.

CHAPTER THREE

MAY BENEFIT BLOOD SUGAR CONTROL

High-fiber food sources assist with easing back assimilation, which might assist with settling your glucose levels by easing back the retention of sugar into your circulatory system

As a matter of fact, a few examinations have shown that fiber might assist with directing glucose and insulin levels. Insulin is a chemical that assists transport with blooding sugar into your cells and guides your body to consume it for energy or store it as fat.

Keeping glucose levels moderate is significant, as spikes in glucose can harm your body over the long run and may prompt sicknesses like diabetes.

One review in 19 individuals with type 2 diabetes investigated the impacts of having a fiber-rich breakfast on glucose levels.

The people who had a high-fiber breakfast that included 9-10 grams of fiber had fundamentally lower post-supper glucose than the individuals who consumed a low-fiber breakfast containing just 2-3 grams of fiber.

Additionally, a review in 20 overweight grown-ups found that the people who consumed something like 8 grams of fiber at breakfast had lower post-dinner insulin levels.

Keeping up with low insulin levels may likewise assist you with shedding pounds by diminishing the quantity of calories your body stores as fat.

Roughage diminish cholesterol and pulse levels

Dietary fiber might assist with bringing down elevated cholesterol and pulse levels, the two of which are risk factors for coronary illness.

One 28-day concentrates on analyzed the heart-sound impacts of eating fiber in 80 individuals with elevated cholesterol.

Analysts saw that individuals who ate 3 grams of dissolvable fiber everyday from oats encountered a 62% decrease in all out cholesterol and a 65% decrease in LDL (terrible) cholesterol, contrasted with a benchmark group.

In an additional 4-week study, 345 individuals ate 3-4 grams of beta-glucan, a dissolvable fiber found in oats, everyday. This gathering experienced critical decreases in LDL (awful) cholesterol, contrasted with a benchmark group.

Besides, eating fiber might diminish your pulse.

An audit of 28 examinations noticed that individuals who ate slims down higher in beta-glucan, a sort of fiber found in oats, had lower pulse than the people who consumed eats less lower in this fiber.

Until now, a large portion of the examination on fiber and pulse has zeroed in on the impacts of fiber supplements - not the fiber in food. Subsequently, more examination is required

CHAPTER FOUR

FOOD SOURCES HIGH IN ROUGHAGE

Fiber, or roughage, is found in practically all plant food varieties, including entire grains, organic products, vegetables, beans, nuts, and seeds.

Be that as it may, a portion of these food varieties are normally higher in roughage than others. Here are the absolute best wellsprings of roughage:

Chiai seeds: 10 grams for every 2-tablespoon (28-gram) serving Lentils: 8 grams for each 1/2-cup (96-gram) serving

Dark beans: 8 grams for every 1/2-cup (86-gram) serving

Lima beans: 7 grams for each 1/2-cup (92-gram) serving.

Chickpeas: 7 grams for each 1/2-cup (82-gram) serving.

Wheat grain: 6 grams for each 1/4-cup (15-gram) serving.

Kidney beans: 6 grams for every 1/2-cup (125-gram) serving.

Flax seeds: 6 grams for each 2-tablespoon (22-gram) serving.

Pears: 6 grams for each medium (178-gram) pea.

Avocado: 5 grams for each 1/2 avocado (68 grams).

Oats: 4 grams for each 1/2-cup (40-gram) uncooked serving.

Apples: 4 grams for each medium (182-gram) apple

Raspberries: 4 grams for each 1/2-cup (62-gram) serving.

Quinoa: 3 grams for each 1/2-cup (93-gram) cooked serving.

Almonds: 3 grams for each 1-ounce (28-gram) serving.

Green beans: 3 grams for each 1-cup (100-gram) serving.

Corn: 3 grams for every 1 huge ear (143 grams).

These food varieties are especially high in roughage, yet numerous other entire food varieties can assist you with expanding your fiber consumption as well.

Essentially trying to incorporate more vegetables, natural products, nuts, seeds, beans, and entire grains in your eating regimen is a brilliant method for expanding your fiber admission and work on your general wellbeing.

How much fiber should i eat per day

Suggested everyday admission of fiber each day

As per the American Heart Association, the day to day incentive for fiber is 25 grams each day on a 2,000-calorie diet for grown-ups. This number may likewise rely upon age or sex:

Ladies under 50: 21 to 25 grams each day

Men under 50: 30 to 38 grams each day

Kids between ages 1 and 18 ought to eat 14 to 31 grams of fiber each day, contingent upon their age and sex. Much higher fiber admissions, found in nations all over the planet, may essentially decrease constant sickness risk.

Fiber accomplishes stomach related snort work however doesn't get a similar style as vitamin D, calcium, and different supplements. It's critical to get the perfect sum fiber to keep your stomach related framework moving along as planned. It likewise gives a great deal of medical advantages past assimilation, like assistance with weight reduction and adjusting stomach microscopic organisms.

The normal American eats something like 16 grams of fiber each day. That is a considerable amount not exactly the everyday suggested admission for a many individuals.

CHAPTER FIVE

FUNDAMENTAL FIBER FOR YOUR HEALTH

All in all, fiber conveys a ton of medical **advantages:**

- upholds weight reduction
- decreases cholesterol and glucose levels
- brings down hazard of cardiovascular sicknesses like stroke, coronary illness, and the sky is the limit from there
- forestalls diabetes
- expands stomach related and gut wellbeing

- powers solid stomach microbes

As a rule, dietary fiber is an umbrella term for the pieces of plants and different food varieties that the body can't process. Rather than separating fiber, fiber goes through your framework and facilitates side effects like clogging. It's essential to eat a wide assortment of food varieties as opposed to depending on one hotspot for fiber consumption.

Instructions to increase your fiber intake

The most effective way to get fiber - while not devouring an excessive number of calories - is to eat high-fiber food varieties. Most vegetables, natural products, and plant-based food sources have fiber. Assuming that your body is gradually changing in accordance with more fiber, spread out your parts between suppers as opposed to eating a ton in a solitary serving.

Food varieties containing high-fiber

It's ideal to add fiber to the eating routine progressively. You would rather not surprise your framework with an excessive amount of mass. "Begin low, go sluggish," as the International

Foundation for Functional Gastrointestinal Disorders puts it. A few ways to include fiber, however not to an extreme, **are:**

- Eat entire organic products like pears and apples as opposed to drinking natural product juices.
- Trade in entire grain assortments rather than white rice, bread, and ordinary pasta.
- Nibble on vegetables rather than pretzels and chips.
- Eat beans and lentils every day.

- Sprinkle china seeds on oat, smoothies, or mixed greens.
- Ensure you're drinking a lot of water when you eat stringy food.

You may likewise find it accommodating to follow the food sources you eat and take note of the fiber content to more readily comprehend the amount you're really eating. Certain individuals attempting to eat sufficient fiber might need to consider taking a fiber supplement.

All things considered, a lot of fiber can likewise be something awful. Furthermore, your body will make some noise (in a real sense and metaphorically) with an assortment of side effects on the off chance that you're eating a lot of it. Fiber supplements have additionally not demonstrated to be close essentially as useful as eating high-fiber food varieties.

CHAPTER SIX

SIDE EFFECTS OF TOO MUCH FIBER

Fiber is otherwise called "mass" or "roughage," and it can make some commotion as it goes through the stomach and digestive organs. On the off chance that you eat in excess of 70 grams per day, your body will start to advise you to ease off.

Signs and side effects:

- Gas
- Bulging
- Blockage
- loose bowels
- stomach squeezing

There's another issue with fiber over-burden. Fiber can tie to significant minerals like calcium, iron, and zinc and keep your framework from engrossing these supplements.

Scale back your fiber consumption assuming you experience these side effects and feel it's because of your eating routine, not any more circumstances like the stomach influenza that has comparable side effects.

On the off chance that you experience serious side effects, converse with your PCP or visit a critical consideration community or the emergency clinic. In intriguing yet genuine cases, a lot of fiber can cause a gastrointestinal (gut) obstacle, which is a blockage that keeps contents from traveling through.

why is fiber good for you

Fiber is one of the principle reasons entire plant food varieties are really great for you.

Developing proof shows that sufficient fiber admission might help your assimilation and diminish your gamble of persistent illness.

A large number of these advantages are interceded by your

stomach miniature biota the large numbers of microorganisms that live in your stomach related framework.

Be that as it may, not all fiber is made equivalent. Various sorts have different wellbeing impacts.

This article makes sense of the proof based medical advantages of fiber diet.

www.ingramcontent.com/pod-product-compliance
Lightning Source LLC
LaVergne TN
LVHW010123170826
845678LV00012B/2577

* 9 7 9 8 8 0 4 7 3 2 1 4 2 *